A Jane Austen Journal

There is nothing I would not do for those who are really my friends. I have no notion of loving people by halves, it is not my nature.

Jane Austen, *Northanger Abbey*

It is a truth universally acknowledged, that a single man in possession of a good fortune, must be in want of a wife.

Jane Austen, **Pride and Prejudice**

There is a stubbornness about me that never can bear to be frightened at the will of others. My courage always rises at every attempt to intimidate me.

—Jane Austen, *Pride and Prejudice*

Time will explain.

Jane Austen, Persuasion

The person, be it gentleman or lady, who has not pleasure in a good novel must be intolerably stupid.

Jane Austen, *Northanger Abbey*

Vanity and pride are different things, though the words are often used synonymously. A person may be proud without being vain. Pride relates more to our opinion of ourselves, vanity to what we would have others think of us.

Jane Austen, Pride and Prejudice

I declare after all there is no enjoyment like reading! How much sooner one tires of anything than of a book! -- When I have a house of my own, I shall be miserable if I have not an excellent library.

Jane Austen, *Pride and Prejudice*

Know your own happiness. You want nothing by patience — or give it a more fascinating name, call it hope.

Jane Austen, **Sense and Sensibility**

Why not seize pleasure at once? How often is happiness destroyed by preparation, foolish preparation!

Jane Austen, *Emma*

Better be without sense than misapply it as you do.

Jane Austen, *Emma*

What dreadful hot weather we have! It keeps one in a continual state of inelegance.

Jane Austen, letter, Sep. 18, 1796

Selfishness must always be forgiven you know, because there is no hope of a cure.

Jane Austen, *Mansfield Park*

Happiness in marriage is entirely a matter of chance. If the dispositions of the parties are ever so well known to each other or ever so similar beforehand, it does not advance their felicity in the least. They always continue to grow sufficiently on afterwards to have their share of vexation; and it is better to know as little as possible of the defects of the person with whom you are to pass your life.

Jane Austen, *Pride and Prejudice*

The more I know of the world, the more I am convinced that I shall never see a man whom I can really love. I require so much!

Jane Austen, *Sense and Sensibility*

My good opinion once lost, is lost forever.

Jane Austen, *Pride and Prejudice*

Think only of the past as its remembrance gives you pleasure.

Jane Austen, Pride and Prejudice

None of us want to be in calm waters all our lives.

Jane Austen, *Persuasion*

I would much rather be merry than wise.

Jane Austen, *Emma*

A woman, especially if she has the misfortune of knowing anything, should conceal it as well as she can.

Jane Austen, *Northanger Abbey*

I will be calm. I will be mistress of myself.

    Jane Austen, Sense and Sensibility

It is particularly incumbent on those who never change their opinion, to be secure of judging properly at first.

Jane Austen, Pride and Prejudice

One half of the world cannot understand the pleasures of the other.

Jane Austen, *Emma*

A lady's imagination is very rapid; it jumps from admiration to love, from love to matrimony in a moment.

— Jane Austen, *Pride and Prejudice*

If adventures will not befall a young lady in her own village, she must seek them abroad.

Jane Austen, *Northanger Abbey*

I must learn to be content with being happier than I deserve.

Jane Austen, *Pride and Prejudice*

It is not every man's fate to marry the woman who loves him best.
                                                        Jane Austen, *Emma*

There could have been no two hearts so open, no tastes so similar, no feelings so in unison.

Jane Austen, *Persuasion*

People always live forever when there is an annuity to be paid them.

> Jane Austen, *Sense and Sensibility*

Indulge your imagination in every possible flight.
                                    Jane Austen, Pride and Prejudice

I am not at all in a humor for writing; I must write on till I am.

Jane Austen, letter to Cassandra Austen, Oct. 26, 1813

Give a girl an education and introduce her properly into the world, and ten to one but she has the means of settling well, without further expense to anybody.

Jane Austen, Mansfield Park

Next week I shall begin my operations on my hat, on which you know my principal hopes of happiness depend.

Jane Austen, letter, Oct. 27, 1798

If I loved you less, I might be able to talk about it more.

Jane Austen, *Emma*

What are men to rocks and mountains?

Jane Austen, Pride and Prejudice

I cannot fix on the hour, or the spot, or the look or the words, which laid the foundation. It is too long ago. I was in the middle before I knew that I had begun.

Jane Austen, Pride and Prejudice

If one scheme of happiness fails, human nature turns to another; if the first calculation is wrong, we make a second better: we find comfort somewhere.

Jane Austen, Mansfield Park

Nothing is more deceitful than the appearance of humility. It is often only carelessness of opinion, and sometimes an indirect boast.

Jane Austen, Pride and Prejudice

Friendship is certainly the finest balm for the pangs of disappointed love.

Jane Austen, **Northanger Abbey**

A large income is the best recipe for happiness I ever heard of.
                                          Jane Austen, Mansfield Park

When pain is over, the remembrance of it often becomes a pleasure.

Jane Austen, Persuasion

One cannot be always laughing at a man without now and then stumbling on something witty.

            Jane Austen, *Pride and Prejudice*

Another stupid party last night; perhaps if larger they might be less intolerable, but here there were only just enough to make one card-table, with six people to look on and talk nonsense to each other.

Jane Austen, letter to Cassandra Austen, May 12, 1801

Laugh as much as you choose, but you will not laugh me out of my opinion.

Jane Austen, *Pride and Prejudice*

A scheme of which every part promises delight, can never be successful; and general disappointment is only warded off by the defense of some little peculiar vexation.

Jane Austen, *Pride and Prejudice*

If any one faculty of our nature may be called more wonderful than the rest, I do think it is memory. There seems something more speakingly incomprehensible in the powers, the failures, the inequalities of memory, than in any other of our intelligences. The memory is sometimes so retentive, so serviceable, so obedient; at others, so bewildered and so weak; and at others again, so tyrannic, so beyond control! We are, to be sure, a miracle every way; but our powers of recollecting and of forgetting do seem peculiarly past finding out.

Jane Austen, Mansfield Park

No man is offended by another man's admiration of the woman he loves; it is the woman only who can make it a torment.

Jane Austen, *Northanger Abbey*

Seldom, very seldom, does complete truth belong to any human disclosure; seldom can it happen that something is not a little disguised or a little mistaken.

— Jane Austen, *Emma*

How quick come the reasons for approving what we like.

Jane Austen, *Persuasion*

For what do we live, but to make sport for our neighbors and laugh at them in our turn?

Jane Austen, *Pride and Prejudice*

Do not give way to useless alarm; though it is right to be prepared for the worst, there is no occasion to look on it as certain.

Jane Austen, Pride and Prejudice

Vanity working on a weak head produces every sort of mischief.

Jane Austen, *Emma*

Surprises are foolish things. The pleasure is not enhanced, and the inconvenience is often considerable.

Jane Austen, *Emma*

He is a gentleman, and I am a gentleman's daughter. So far we are equal.

Jane Austen, *Pride and Prejudice*

People themselves alter so much, that there is something new to be observed in them forever.

Jane Austen, *Pride and Prejudice*

There is, I believe, in every disposition a tendency to some particular evil -- a natural defect, which not even the best education can overcome.

— Jane Austen, *Pride and Prejudice*

From politics, it was an easy step to silence.

Jane Austen, *Northanger Abbey*

Silly things do cease to be silly if they are done by sensible people in an impudent way.

Jane Austen, Emma

I can recollect nothing more to say at present; perhaps breakfast may assist my ideas. I was deceived -- my breakfast supplied only two ideas -- that the rolls were good and the butter bad.

Jane Austen, letter, Jun. 19, 1799

You pierce my soul. I am half agony, half hope.

Jane Austen, *Persuasion*

Mary wished to say something very sensible, but knew not how.

Jane Austen, *Pride and Prejudice*

Life seems but a quick succession of busy nothings.

Jane Austen, *Mansfield Park*

I wish, as well as everybody else, to be perfectly happy; but, like everybody else, it must be in my own way.

Jane Austen, *Sense and Sensibility*

It is not time or opportunity that is to determine intimacy;--it is disposition alone. Seven years would be insufficient to make some people acquainted with each other, and seven days are more than enough for others.

Jane Austen, *Sense and Sensibility*

We are all fools in love.

Jane Austen, Pride and Prejudice

There are people, who the more you do for them, the less they will do for themselves.

Jane Austen, *Emma*

I am only resolved to act in that manner, which will, in my own opinion, constitute my happiness, without reference to you, or to any person so wholly unconnected with me.

Jane Austen, *Pride and Prejudice*

How wonderful, how very wonderful the operations of time, and the changes of the human mind!

Jane Austen, *Mansfield Park*

She was stronger alone

Jane Austen, *Sense and Sensibility*

It is very difficult for the prosperous to be humble.

Jane Austen, *Emma*

One cannot have too large a party.

Jane Austen, *Emma*

We have all a better guide in ourselves, if we would attend to it, than any other person can be.

Jane Austen, *Mansfield Park*

Those who do not complain are never pitied.

Jane Austen, *Pride and Prejudice*

I cannot help thinking that it is more natural to have flowers grow out of the head than fruit.

> Jane Austen, letter to Cassandra Austen, Jun. 11, 1799

Men of sense, whatever you may choose to say, do not want silly wives.

Jane Austen, *Emma*

An engaged woman is always more agreeable than a disengaged. She is satisfied with herself. Her cares are over, and she feels that she may exert all her powers of pleasing without suspicion. All is safe with a lady engaged: no harm can be done.

            Jane Austen, *Mansfield Park*

To be fond of dancing was a certain step towards falling in love.
                                    Jane Austen, Pride and Prejudice

It is well to have as many holds upon happiness as possible.
              Jane Austen, *Northanger Abbey*

Single women have a dreadful propensity for being poor, which is one very strong argument in favour of matrimony.

Jane Austen, letter to Fanny Knight, Mar. 13, 1817

I do not think I ever opened a book in my life which had not something to say upon woman's inconstancy. Songs and proverbs, all talk of woman's fickleness. But perhaps you will say, these were all written by men.

Jane Austen, Persuasion

There is no charm equal to tenderness of heart.

Jane Austen, Emma

One man's ways may be as good as another's, but we all like our own best.

Jane Austen, Persuasion

It will, I believe, be everywhere found, that as the clergy are, or are not what they ought to be, so are the rest of the nation.

Jane Austen, *Mansfield Park*

I do not want people to be very agreeable, as it saves me the trouble of liking them a great deal.

                                                   Jane Austen, letter to Cassandra Austen, Dec. 24, 1798

It would be mortifying to the feelings of many ladies, could they be made to understand how little the heart of a man is affected by what is costly or new in their attire.

Jane Austen, Northanger Abbey

If I could but know his heart, everything would become easy.

Jane Austen, *Sense and Sensibility*

I could easily forgive his pride, if he had not mortified mine.

Jane Austen, *Pride and Prejudice*

There was a monstrous deal of stupid quizzing and common-place nonsense talked, but scarcely any wit.

Jane Austen, letter to Cassandra, April 21, 1805

To sit in the shade on a fine day, and look upon verdure is the most perfect refreshment.

Jane Austen, **Mansfield Park**

Where people are really attached, poverty itself is wealth.

Jane Austen, *Northanger Abbey*

What praise is more valuable than the praise of an intelligent servant?

Jane Austen, *Pride and Prejudice*

The truth is, that in London it is always a sickly season. Nobody is healthy in London, nobody can be.

Jane Austen, *Emma*

I am very much obliged to my dear little George for his messages, for his Love at least--his Duty I suppose was only in consequence of some hint of my favourable intentions towards him from his father or mother. I am sincerely rejoiced however that I ever was born, since it has been the means of procuring him a dish of Tea.

Jane Austen, letter, Dec. 19, 1798

We live entirely in the dressing room now, which I like very much; I always feel so much more elegant in it than in the parlour.

          Jane Austen, letter, Dec. 2, 1798

Expect a most agreeable letter; for not being overburdened with subject (having nothing at all to say) I shall have no check to my Genius from beginning to end.

                    Jane Austen, letter To Cassandra Austen, Jan. 21, 1801

I wrote without much effort; for I was rich, and the rich are always respectable, whatever be their style of writing.
  Jane Austen, letter to Cassandra Austen, Jun. 20, 1808

I have made myself two or three caps to wear of evenings since I came home, and they save me a world of torment as to hairdressing, which at present gives me no trouble beyond washing and brushing, for my long hair is always plaited up out of sight, and my short hair curls well enough to want no papering.

Jane Austen, letter, Dec. 2, 1798

A lady, without a family, was the very best preserver of furniture in the world.

Jane Austen, *Persuasion*

There are such beings in the world -- perhaps one in a thousand -- as the creature you and I should think perfection; where grace and spirit are united to worth, where the manners are equal to the heart and understanding; but such a person may not come in your way, or, if he does, he may not be the eldest son of a man of fortune, the near relation of your particular friend, and belonging to your own county.

Jane Austen, letter to Fanny Knight, Nov. 18, 1814

It must be very improper that a young lady should dream of a gentleman before the gentleman is first known to have dreamt of her.
                                                    Jane Austen, *Northanger Abbey*

It's been many years since I had such an exemplary vegetable.
                                          Jane Austen, Pride and Prejudice

To look almost pretty is an acquisition of higher delight to a girl who has been looking plain for the first fifteen years of her life than a beauty from her cradle can ever receive.

— Jane Austen, *Northanger Abbey*

There certainly are not so many men of large fortune in the world as there are pretty women to deserve them.

Jane Austen, Mansfield Park

James Digweed left Hampshire today. I think he must be in love with you, from his anxiety to have you go to the Faversham Balls & wise from his supposing that the two Elms fell from their grief at your absence. Was it not a galant idea? It never occurred to me before, but I dare say it was so.

     Jane Austen, letter to Cassandra Austen, Nov. 21, 1800

Run mad as often as you choose, but do not faint!

Jane Austen, *Love and Friendship*

Let other pens dwell on guilt and misery.

Jane Austen, *Mansfield Park*

I could not sit seriously down to write a serious romance under any other motive than to save my life; and if it were indispensable for me to keep it up and never relax into laughing at myself or other people, I am sure I should be hung before I had finished the first chapter. No, I must keep to my own style and go on in my own way; and though I may never succeed again in that, I am convinced that I should totally fail in any other.

Jane Austen, letter to Mr. Clarke, Apr. 1, 1816

Could there be finer symptoms? Is not general incivility the very essence of love?

Jane Austen, *Pride and Prejudice*

I am sorry to tell you that I am getting very extravagant, and spending all my money, and, what is worse for you, I have been spending yours too.

       Jane Austen, letter to Cassandra Austen, Apr. 18, 1811

That sanguine expectation of happiness which is happiness itself.

Jane Austen, *Sense and Sensibility*

The mere habit of learning to love is the thing; and a teachableness of disposition in a young lady is a great blessing.

Jane Austen, **Northanger Abbey**

It is only a novel ... or, in short, only some work in which the greatest powers of the mind are displayed, in which the most thorough knowledge of human nature, the happiest delineation of its varieties, the liveliest effusions of wit and humour, are conveyed to the world in the best-chosen language.

Jane Austen, Northanger Abbey

Let us leave it to the reviewers to abuse such effusions of fancy at their leisure, and over every new novel to talk in threadbare strains of the trash with which the press now groans. Let us not desert one another; we are an injured body.

Jane Austen, Northanger Abbey

We all know him to be a proud, unpleasant sort of man; but this would be nothing if you really liked him.

Jane Austen, *Pride and Prejudice*

Printed in Great Britain
by Amazon